ISBN 978-1-333-60186-7
PIBN 10525013

Price, 25 Cents.

ABSTRACT OF COLENSO

ON THE

PENTATEUCH:

A comprehensive summary of Bishop Colenso's argument, proving that the Pentateuch is not historically true ; and that it is composed by several writers, the earliest of whom lived in the time of Samuel, from 1100 to 1060 B. C., and the latest the time of Jeremiah, from 641 to 624 B. C.

TO WHICH IS APPENDED AN ESSAY ON

HE NATION and COUNTRY of the JEWS.

"hey do the greatest injury to religion who endeavor to establish it upon a false basis."

New York:

SOLD BY THE

AMERICAN NEWS COMPANY.

1871

ABSTRACT OF COLENSO

ON THE

PENTATEUCH:

A COMPREHENSIVE SUMMARY OF BISHOP COLENSO'S ARGU-
MENT, PROVING THAT THE PENTATEUCH IS NOT HISTORI-
CALLY TRUE; AND THAT IT WAS COMPOSED BY SEVERAL
WRITERS, THE EARLIEST OF WHOM LIVED IN THE TIME OF
SAMUEL, FROM 1100 TO 1060 B. C., AND THE LATEST IN THE
TIME OF JEREMIAH, FROM 641 TO 624 B. C.

PREFACE.

THE author of the book of which this pamphlet is an abstract is not an Infidel, but a Bishop of the Church of England,
having charge of the Diocese of Natal, in South Africa. While
engaged in the translation of the Scriptures into the Zulu tongue,
with the aid of intelligent natives, he was brought face to face
with questions which in former days had caused him some uneasi-
ness, but with respect to which he had been enabled to satisfy his
mind sufficiently for practical purposes, as a Christian minister,
by means of the specious explanations given in most commenta-
ries on the Bible, and had settled down into a willing acquies-
cence in the general truth of the narrative of the Old Testament,
whatever difficulties might still hang about particular parts of it.

But while translating the story of the Flood, a simple-minded but intelligent native, with the docility of a child but the reasoning powers of mature age, looked up and asked: "Is all that true? Do you really believe that all the beasts, birds, and creeping things, from hot countries and cold, came thus by pairs and entered Noah's ark? And did Noah gather food for them all; for the beasts and birds of prey as well as the rest?" The Bishop had recently acquired sufficient knowledge of geology to know that a universal Deluge, such as is described in Genesis, could not have taken place. So his heart answered in the words of the Prophet, "Shall a man speak lies in the name of the Lord?" (Zech. xiii., 3.) He dared not do so, but gave the brother such a reply as satisfied him for the time, without throwing any discredit upon the general veracity of the Bible history. But being driven to search more deeply into these questions, the Bishop wrote to a friend in England to send him the best books on both sides of the question of the credibility of the Mosaic history. His friend sent him the works of Ewald and Kurtz, the former in German and the latter in an English translation. Laying Ewald on the shelf, he studied Kurtz, who maintained with great zeal and ability the historical accuracy of the Pentateuch. He then grappled with Ewald, who maintained an opposite view. The result of the Bishop's study, with the aid of a few other German books, appeared in the first volume of his work issued in 1862, followed soon after by four more volumes. The books met with a very large sale in England. The first two volumes only are published as yet in this country. Perhaps the demand would not encourage the republication of the complete set. A great deal of the work is made up of apology, much more of answers to orthodox expositors and critics who have attempted to explain the very difficulties which presented themselves to the inquiring mind of the author, and a large part of the last three volumes consists of elaborate criticism, and a presentation of various portions of the Pentateuch attributed to the different writers thereof. In this Abstract all those portions are passed by, the object being to compress into the smallest practicable compass the gist of the whole argument. Should the reader wish to see what can be said in answer to the very criticisms which Colenso makes, he will find it fairly presented and candidly considered by the author in his complete work.

INCREDIBLE NARRATIVES OF THE PENTATEUCH.

IN Vol. I. Bishop Colenso shows, by means of a number of prominent instances, that the books of the Pentateuch contain, in their own account of the story which they profess to relate, such remarkable contradictions, and involve such plain impossibilities, that they cannot be regarded as true narratives of actual historical matters of fact. Passing over the many difficulties which exist in the earlier parts of the history, he begins at once with the account of the Exodus.

. THE FAMILY OF JUDAH.

Judah was forty-two years old when he went down with Jacob into Egypt, being three years older than his brother Joseph, who was then thirty-nine. For " Joseph was thirty years old when he stood before Pharaoh " (G. xli. 46) ; and from that time nine years elapsed (seven of plenty and two of famine) before Jacob came down into Egypt. Judah was born in the fourth year of Jacob's double marriage (G. xxix. 35), being the fourth of the seven children of Leah born in seven years ; and Joseph was born of Rachel in the seventh year (G. xxx. 24, 26 ; xxi. 41). In these forty-two years of Judah's life the following events are recorded in G. xxxviii. :

He grows up, marries, and has three sons. The eldest grows up, marries, and dies. The second son marries his brother's widow and dies. The third son, after waiting to grow to maturity, declines to marry the widow. The widow then deceives Judah himself, and bears him twins—Pharez and Zarah. One of these twins grows up and has two sons—Hezron and Hamul—born to him before Jacob goes down into Egypt.

ALL THE PEOPLE AT THE DOOR OF THE TABERNACLE.

Moses, at the command of Jehovah, gathered " all the congregation together unto the door of the tabernacle." (L. viii. 1-4.)

By "all the congregation" is meant the whole body of the people, or at all events the main body of adult males in the prime of life, as is shown by numerous texts where the expression is used. (E. xvi. 2; L. xxiv. 14; N. i. 18.) In Jo. viii. 35, the women and children are included. The mass of the male adults must have numbered more than the number of warriors, which is nowhere fixed at less than 600,000. Now the whole width of the tabernacle was only eighteen feet, as may be gathered from E. xxvi., so that a close column of 600,000 men covering this front, allowing two feet in width and eighteen inches in depth for each full-grown man, would have reached back nearly twenty miles; or if the column covered the whole width of the court, which was ninety feet, it would have extended back nearly four miles. The whole court of the tabernacle comprised not more than 1,692 square yards, after deducting the area of the tabernacle itself, which covered 108 square yards, and therefore could have held only 5,000 people closely packed. The ministering Levites "from thirty to fifty years old" numbered 8,580 (N. iv. 48); even they, consequently, could not all have stood within the court.

MOSES AND JOSHUA ADDRESSING ALL ISRAEL.

"These be the words which Moses spake unto all Israel." (D. i. 1.)

"And Moses called all Israel and said unto them." (D. v. 1.)

"There was not a word of all that Moses commanded, which Joshua read not before all the congregation of Israel, with the women, and the little ones, and the strangers that were conversant among them." (Jo. viii. 35.)

How was it possible to do this before at least 2,000,000 people? Could Moses or Joshua, as actual eye-witnesses, have expressed themselves in such extravagant language? Surely not.

EXTENT OF THE CAMP AND DUTIES OF THE PRIESTS.

The camp of the Israelites must have been at least a mile and a half in diameter. This would be allowing to each person on the average a space three times the size of a coffin for a full-grown man. The ashes, offal, and refuse of the sacrifices would therefore have to be carried by the priest in person a distance of three-quarters of a mile "without the camp, unto a clean place." (L. iv. 11, 12.) There were only three priests, namely, Aaron,

Eleazer, and Ithamar, to do all this work for 2,000,000 people. All the wood and water would have to be brought into this immense camp from the outside. Where could the supplies have been got while the camp was under Sinai, in a desert, for nearly twelve months together? How could so great a camp have been kept clean?

But how huge does the difficulty become if we take the more reasonable dimensions of twelve miles square for this camp; that is, about the size of London! Imagine at least half a million of men having to go out daily a distance of six miles and back, to the suburbs, for the common necessities of nature, as the law directed.

TWO NUMBERINGS SIX MONTHS APART; EXACT COINCIDENCE.

In E. xxx. 11-13, Jehovah commanded Moses to take a census of the children of Israel, and in doing it to collect half a shekel of the sanctuary as atonement money. This expression " shekel of the sanctuary " is put into the mouth of Jehovah six or seven months before the tabernacle was made. In E. xxxviii. 26, we read of such a tribute being paid, but nothing is there said of any *census* being taken, only the number of those who paid, from twenty years old and upward, was 603,550 men. In N. i. 1-46, more than six months after this occasion, an account of an actual census is given, but no *atonement money* is mentioned. If in the first instance a census was taken, but accidentally omitted to be mentioned, and in the second instance the tribute was paid but accidentally omitted likewise, it is nevertheless surprising that the number of adult males should have been identically the same (603,550) on both occasions, six months apart.

THE ISRAELITES DWELLING IN TENTS.

The Israelites at their exodus were provided with tents (E. xvi. 16), in which they undoubtedly encamped and dwelt. They did not dwell in tents in Egypt, but in " houses " with " doors," " sideposts," and " lintels." These tents must have been made either of hair or of skin (E. xxvi. 7, 14, xxxvi. 14, 19)—more probably of the latter—and were therefore much heavier than the modern canvas tents. At least 200,000 were required to accommodate 2,000,000 people. Supposing they took these tents from Egypt, how did they carry them in their hurried march to the Red Sea?

The people had burdens enough without them. They had to carry their kneading troughs with the dough unleavened, their clothes, their cooking utensils, couches, infants, aged and infirm persons, and food enough for at least a month's use, or until manna was provided for them in the wilderness, which was "on the fifteenth day of the second month after their departure out of the land of Egypt". (E. xvi. 1.). One of these tents, with its poles, pegs, etc., would be a load for a single ox, so that they would have needed 200,000 oxen to carry the tents. But oxen are not usually trained to carry goods on their backs, and will not do so without training.

THE ISRAELITES ARMED.

"The children of Israel went up harnessed out of the land of Egypt." (E. xiii. 18.)

The marginal reading for "harnessed" is "by five in rank." But as this would make of the 600,000 men a column sixty-eight miles long, this translation only increases the difficulty, as it would have taken several days to have started them all off. The Hebrew word is elsewhere rendered "armed," or "in battle array." Certainly about a month after the exodus the Israelites "discomfited" the Amalekites "with the edge of the sword." (E. xvii. 13.) Hence they somehow possessed arms. And yet this army of 600,000 had become so debased by long servitude that they could not strike a single blow for liberty in Egypt, but could only weakly wail and murmur against Moses, saying, "It had been better for us to serve the Egyptians than that we should die in the wilderness!"

INSTITUTION OF THE PASSOVER.

The whole population of Israel were instructed in one single day to keep the passover, and actually did keep it. (E. xii.) At the first notice of any such feast, Jehovah said, "I will pass through the land of Egypt *this night.*" The passover was to be killed "*at even*" on the same day that Moses received the command. The women were at the same time ordered to borrow jewels of their neighbors, the Egyptians. After midnight of the same day the Israelites received notice to start for the wilderness. No one was to go out of his house till morning, when they were to take their hurried flight with their cattle and herds. How could 2,000,000 people, scattered about over a wide district as they must have been with their cattle and herds, have gotten ready and taken a simultaneous hurried flight at twelve hours' notice?

MARCH OUT OF EGYPT.

The Israelites, with their flocks and herds, reached the Red Sea, a distance of from fifty to sixty miles over a sandy desert in three days! Marching fifty abreast, the able-bodied warriors alone would have filled up the road for seven miles, and the whole multitude would have made a column twenty-two miles long, so that the last of the body could not have been started until the front had advanced that distance—more than two days' journey for such a mixed company. Then the sheep and cattle must have formed another vast column, covering a much greater tract of ground in proportion to their number. Upon what did these two millions of sheep and oxen feed in the journey to the Red Sea over a desert region, sandy, gravelly, and stony alternately? How did the people manage with the sick and infirm, and especially with the 750 births that must have taken place in the three days' march?

THE SHEEP AND CATTLE IN THE WILDERNESS.

The Israelites undoubtedly had flocks and herds of cattle. (E. xxxiv. 3.) They sojourned nearly a year before Sinai, where there was no feed for cattle; and the wilderness in which they sojourned nearly forty years is now and was then a desert. (D. xxxii. 10; viii. 15.) The cattle surely did not subsist on manna!

EXTENT AND POPULATION OF THE LAND OF CANAAN.

The extent of land occupied by the Israelites in the time of Joshua was about 11,000 square miles, or 7,000,000 acres—a little larger than the State of Vermont. The number of Israelites was not less than 2,000,000. This limited, mountainous, and by no means fertile area of country, therefore, had to subsist these 2,000,000 people, and prior to their occupation of it had subsisted " *seven nations greater and mightier* " than the Israelitish nation itself. (D. vii. 1.)

FECUNDITY OF THE HEBREW MOTHERS.

" All the first-born males from a month old and upwards, of
those that were numbered, were 22,273." (N. iii. 43.) The lowest
computation of the whole number of the people at that time is
2,000,000. The number of males would be 1,000,000. Dividing
the latter number by the number of first born gives 44, which
would be the average number of boys in each family, or about
88 children by each mother. Or, if where the first born were
females the males were not counted, the number of children by
each mother would be reduced to 44.

PRODIGIOUS INCREASE IN FOUR GENERATIONS.

The number of the children of Israel who went into Egypt
was 70 (E. i. 5). They sojourned in Egypt 215 years. It could
not have been 430 years, as would appear from E. xii. 40. The
marginal chronology makes the period 215 years, and there were
only four generations to the exodus, namely, Levi, Kohath, Am-
ram, and Moses (E. vi. 16, 18, 20). How could these people have
increased in 215 years from 70 souls so as to number 600,000 warriors? It would have required an average number of 46 children
to each father. The 12 sons of Jacob had between them only 53
sons. At this rate of increase, in the fourth generation there
would have been only 6,311 males, provided they were all living
at the time of the exodus, instead of 1,000,000. If we add the
fifth generation, who would be mostly children, the total number
of males would not have exceeded 28,465.

EXTRAORDINARY INCREASE OF THE DANITES.

Dan in the first generation had but one son (G. xlvi. 23), and
yet in the fourth generation his descendants had increased to
62,700 warriors (N. ii. 26), or 64,400 (N. xxvi. 43). Each of his
sons and grandsons must have had about 80 children of both
sexes. On the other hand, the Levites increased the number of
" males from a month old and upwards " during the 38 years in
the wilderness only from 22,000 to 23,000 (N. iii. 39, xxvi. 62)
and the tribe of Manasseh during the same time increased from
32,200 (N. i. 35) to 52,700 (xxvi. 34).

IMPOSSIBLE DUTIES OF THE PRIESTS.

Aaron and his two sons were the only priests during Aaron's

lifetime. They had to make all the burnt offerings on a single altar nine feet square (E. xxxvii. 1), besides attending to other priestly duties for 2,000,000 people. At the birth of every child, both a burnt offering and a sin offering had to be made. The number of births must be reckoned at least 250 a day, for which consequently 500 sacrifices would have to be offered daily —an impossible duty to be performed by three priests. For poor women pigeons were accepted instead of lambs. If half of them offered pigeons, and only one instead of two, it would have required 90,000 pigeons annually for this purpose alone. Where did they get the pigeons? How could they have had them at all under Sinai? There were thirteen cities where the presence of these three priests was required (Jo. xxi. 19). The three priests had to eat a large portion of the burnt offerings (N. xviii. 10) and all the sin offerings—250 pigeons a day—more than 80 for each priest.

IMPOSSIBLE SACRIFICES AT THE PASSOVER.

In keeping the second passover under Sinai, 150,000 lambs must have been killed, i. e., one for each family (E. xii. 3, 4). The Levites slew them, and the three priests had to sprinkle the blood from their hands (1 Chr. xxx. 16, xxxv. 11). The killing had to be done "between two evenings" (E. xii. 6), and the sprinkling had to be done in about two hours. The killing must have been done in the court of the tabernacle (L. i. 3, 5, xvii. 2-6). The area of the court could have held but 5,000 people at most. Here the lambs had to be sacrificed at the rate of 1,250 a minute, and each of the three priests had to sprinkle the blood of more than 400 lambs every minute for two hours.

INCREDIBLE SLAUGHTER.

The number of warriors of the Israelites, as recorded at the exodus, was 600,000 (E. xii. 37); subsequently it was 603,550 (E. xxxviii. 25-28), and at the end of their wanderings it was 601,730 (N. xxvi. 51). But in 2 Chr. xiii. 3 Abijah, king of Judah, brings 400,000 men against Jeroboam, king of Israel, with 800,000, and " there fell down slain of Israel 500,000 chosen men " (v. 17). On another occasion, Pekah, king of Israel, slew of Judah in one day 120,000 valiant men (2 Chr. xxviii. 6.)

UNPARALLELED PRODIGY OF VALOR.

Among other prodigies of valor, 12,000 Israelites are recorded
in N. xxxi. as slaying all the male Midianites, taking captive all
the females and children, seizing all their cattle and flocks, num-
bering 808,000 head, taking all their goods and burning all their
cities, without the loss of a single man.   Then they killed all the
women and children except 32,000 virgins, whom they kept for
themselves.   There would seem to have been at least 80,000
females in the aggregate, of whom 48,000 were killed, besides
(say) 20,000 boys.   The number of men slaughtered must have
been about 48,000.   Each Israelite therefore must have killed four
men in battle, carried off eight captive women and children, and
driven home sixty-seven head of cattle.   And then after reaching
home, as a pastime, by command of Moses, he had to murder six
of his captive women and children in cold blood.

VOL. II.

IRRECONCILABLE DIFFICULTIES.

IN vol. II. Bishop Colenso devotes a preface and a first chapter
to the maintenance of the criticisms of vol. I.   He shows that it
is impossible to apply any system of reduction to the exaggerated
numbers given in every part of the Pentateuch, without encoun-
tering difficulties and contradictions quite as formidable as those
presented by him.   He then proceeds to investigate the question
of the real origin, age, and authorship of the different portions of
the Pentateuch and other early books of the Bible, and makes the
following points :

CONTRADICTORY STORY OF THE CREATION AND DELUGE.

The cosmogony of the 2d chapter of Genesis is contradictory
to that of chapter 1 in six particulars, the chief of which is, that
in the first chapter the birds and beasts are created before man,
and in the second after man.   Again, in the first account Adam
and Eve are created together, completing the work of creation,
and in the second man is first made, then the beasts and birds,

and lastly woman. It is therefore apparent that the two accounts were written by different men; and this is corroborated by the use of the name Lord God (Jehovah Elohim) in chapter 2, while in chapter 1 it is simply God (Elohim). A similar criticism is applied to the story of the flood, which is evidently composed by two different writers, one making Noah take into the ark animals of every kind, including clean beasts, by twos (G. vii. 8, 9), and the other making him take in the clean beasts by sevens (v. 2, 5). In this story, as in that of the creation, one writer uses the name of God simply, and the other Lord God.

ELOHISTIC AND JEHOVISTIC WRITERS.

The book of Genesis bears evidence throughout of being the work of two different writers, one of whom is distinguished by the constant use of the word Elohim (translated " God "), and the other by the admixture with it of the name Jehovah (translated "Lord "). The Elohistic passages, taken together, form a very tolerably connected whole, only interrupted here and there by a break caused apparently by the Jehovistic writer having removed some part of the Elohistic narrative, replacing it, perhaps, by one of his own. Thus there are two contradictory accounts of the creation and of the deluge intermingled.

THE PENTATEUCH COMPOSED LONG AFTER MOSES'S DEATH.

The books of the Pentateuch are never ascribed to Moses in the inscriptions of Hebrew manuscripts, or anywhere else, except in our modern translations. They must have been composed at a later age than that of Moses or Joshua, as is shown by numerous passages that speak of places and things by names that were not known nor given till long after the death of these men. For example, Gilgal, mentioned in D. xi. 30, was not given as the name of that place till after the entrance into Canaan (Jo. v. 9). Dan, mentioned in G. xiv. 14, was not so called till long after the time of Moses (Jo. xix. 47). In G. xxxvi. 31, the beginning of the reign of kings over Israel is spoken of historically, an event which did not occur before the time of Samuel.

THE BOOK OF JOSHUA WRITTEN IN DAVID'S LIFETIME.

In Josh. x. 12-14, the miracle of the sun and moon standing

still is recorded, and in verse 13 these words are found: "Is not this written in the Book of Jasher?" Now, in 2 Sam. i. 18, we read that David " bade them teach the children of Judah the use of the bow. Behold, it is written in the book of Jasher." The natural inference is, that this book was written not earlier than the time of David, and the above passage in the book of Joshua was written of course after that.

THE BOOKS OF KINGS WRITTEN AS LATE AS 561 B. C.

The Books of Kings seem to have been written as late, at least, as 561 B. C., because in 2 Kings xxv. 27–30, mention is made of Evil-merodach, king of Babylon, taking Jehoiachin, king of Judah, out of prison, and feeding him "all the days of his life." Evil-merodach came to the throne 561 B. C., and reigned two years.

THE CHRONICLES WRITTEN ABOUT 400 B. C.

The author of the Books of Chronicles was probably a priest or Levite, who wrote about 400 B. C. or nearly 200 years after the captivity, and 650 years after David came to the throne. These books go over the same grounds as the books of Samuel and Kings, and often in the very same words. The Chronicles are very inaccurate, and often contradictory to Samuel and Kings. In 1 Chr. iii. 19–21, we have the following genealogy : Zerubbabel, Hananiah, Pelatiah ; so that the Book was written after the birth of Zerubbabel's grandson, and Zerubbabel was the leader of the expedition which returned to Jerusalem after the decree of Cyrus, 536 B. C.

EZRA AND NEHEMIAH WRITTEN AFTER 456 B. C.

The Books of Ezra and Nehemiah were, of course, written after 456 B. C., when Ezra arrived at Jerusalem. Nehemiah's last act of reformation was in 409 B. C., and yet in Neh. xii. 11, we have given the genealogy of Jaddua, who was high priest in Alexander's time, 332 B. C.

FIRST INTRODUCTION OF THE NAME JEHOVAH.

In E. vi. 2–8, God says to Moses : " By my name Jehovah was. I not known to them " (the patriarchs), and yet the name Jehovah, translated Lord, is repeatedly used in the book of Genesis. If

the name originated in the days of Moses, he certainly would
not, in writing the story of the Pentateuch, have put it into the
mouths of the patriarchs, Abraham, Isaac, and Jacob (G. xiv. 22,
xxvi. 22, xxviii. 16), much less into that of a heathen man,
Abimelech (xxvi. 28). The contradiction is explained by the fact
that two different writers were concerned in composing the narrative, one of whom, in speaking of God, uses the name Elohim,
and the other the name Jehovah. The ground-work of the Pentateuch (and but a small portion of it, as the Bishop proposes to
show hereafter) was composed before the name Jehovah had been
familiar.

SAMUEL PROBABLY THE ELOHISTIC WRITER.

During and after the time of Samuel, we observe in the books
known by his name a gradually increasing partiality for the use
of names compounded with Jehovah (*jo* or *iah*), while there is
no instance of the kind throughout the Book of Judges, which
contains numerous names compounded with Elohim (*el*). In the
first seven chapters of the first Book of Samuel we find the following names compounded with Elohim : *El*kanah, *El*ihu, *El*i, Sam-
u*el*, *El*eazer ; while we meet with but one name compounded with
Jehovah, viz : *Jo*shua (vi. 18). But this name evidently belongs to
a man living considerably later than the time of Samuel, for the
passage reads, " which stone remaineth unto this day in the field
of Joshua." Then we read in viii. 1, 2, " When Samuel was old,
he made his sons judges over Israel; now the name of his first-
born was *Jo*el, and the name of his second Ab*iah*." It is remarkable that his first-born son should be named *Jo*el, a contraction
of the compound name Jehovah and Elohim. In 1 Chr. vi. 28,
we are told that the name of Samuel's eldest son was Vashni.
From this it would seem that the name was afterwards changed
to Joel. In the subsequent chapters there is a gradual increase
of names compounded with Jehovah.

In the Elohistic portions of the Book of Genesis, in some
of which a multitude of names occur, and many of them compounded with Elohim, in the form of *El*, there is not a single
one compounded with Jehovah, in the form either of the prefix
Jeho or *Jo*, or the termination *jah*, both of which were so com-
monly employed in the later times. The name Jehovah is first

introduced by the Elohistic writer in Ex. vi. 3, as a *new* name for the God of Israel.

From these and other evidences adduced, Bishop Colenso concludes with some degree of confidence that Samuel was the Elohistic writer of the Pentateuch, and that the Jehovistic writer must have written not earlier than the latter part of David's life, when the name of Jehovah had become quite common, and names began to be compounded with it freely. The narrative being written from 300 to 400 years after the death of Moses, could not, therefore, have been historically true, but may have been intended as a series of parables, based on legendary facts, some of which, perhaps, had been recorded from time to time in a roll deposited in the temple archives, to which access was occasionally had by the priests.

[NOTE.—Sir Isaac Newton, in his "Observations upon the Prophecies," etc., concludes that Samuel put the books of Moses and Joshua into the form now extant, inserting into the book of Genesis (xxxvi. 31–39) the race of the kings of Edom.]

VOL. III.

THE AUTHOR OF DEUTERONOMY.

In vol. III., Bishop Colenso presents in great detail arguments to prove that the book of Deuteronomy was written by a different hand from that or those which wrote the rest of the Pentateuch. No attentive reader of the Bible, he says, can have failed to remark the striking difference which exists between the style and contents of Deuteronomy and those of the other books generally of the Pentateuch. Deuteronomy forms the living portion, the sum and substance, of the whole Pentateuch. When we speak of the "law of Moses," we speak of Deuteronomy. In the New Testament Deuteronomy is frequently quoted with emphasis as the law of Moses.

The principal proofs of a different authorship of this book are as follows :

1. Each writer distinctly professes to give the identical commandments as *spoken* (E. xx. 11) or *written* (D. v. 22) by Jehovah ;

but each assigns an entirely different reason for the observance of the Sabbath. In Exodus it is because God rested on the seventh day ; in Deuteronomy it is because he brought the Israelites out of Egypt "through a mighty hand and by a stretched out arm." It is remarkable that the Deuteronomist should ignore the reason assigned in Exodus.

2. In the other books of the Pentateuch, the priests are *always* styled the "sons of Aaron" (L. i. 5, 7, 8, 11, ii. 2, iii. 2, xiii. 2 ; N. x. 8 ; comp. L. xxi. 21), and never the "sons of Levi." In Deuteronomy they are always called "sons of Levi," or "Levites" (D. xvii. 9, 18, xviii. 1, xxi. 5, xxiv. 8, xxvii. 9, xxxi. 9 ; comp. xviii. 1, 5), and never "sons of Aaron."

3. The Deuteronomist, in using the word "law," invariably refers to the *whole* law (D. i. 5, iv. 8, 44, xvii. 11, 18, 19, xxvii. 3, 8, 26) ; the other books almost always use the words with reference to particular laws (E. xii. 49 ; L. vi. 9, 14, 25, vii. 1, 7, 11, 37).

4. The Deuteronomist confines all sacrifices to one place "which Jehovah would choose," "to put his name there" (D. xii. 5, 11, 14, 18, 21, 26) ; the other books say nothing about this, but expressly imply the contrary (E. xx. 24).

5. The Deuteronomist, though he strictly enjoins the observance of the other three great feasts, and the Passover (xvi. 1–17), makes no mention whatever of the Feast of Trumpets (L. xxiii. 23–25, N. xxix. 1–6), or the Day of Atonement (L. xxiii. 26–32, N. xxix. 7–11), on each of which days it was expressly ordered that the people should "do no servile work," but should hold "a holy convocation." The directions in N. xxix are supposed to have been laid down by Jehovah only a few weeks previous to the address of Moses in Deuteronomy ; yet here in making a final summary of duties, as he is represented as doing, he omits all mention of those two important days, upon which the same stress is laid in L. xxiii. as on the other three great feasts, and for the neglect of which death was threatened as a punishment.

6. In D. viii. 4, xxix. 5, and elsewhere, mention is made of clothing which lasted the Israelites forty years without waxing old upon them. No mention is made in the older narrative of this miraculous provision of clothing.

7. In D. ix. 18, Moses says he "fell down before the Lord as at the first forty days and nights," and fasted as he had done also at the first (*v.* 9). According to the older story, he fasted only

when he went up the second time—not the first (E. xxiv. 18, xxxiv. 28).

8. In E. xviii. 25, 26, we read that Moses chose able men out of all Israel, and made them judges over the people. This was just before the giving of the law at Sinai. In D. i. 6–18, the appointment of these same officers is made to take place nearly twelve months after the giving of the law, when the Israelites are just about to leave Horeb (v. 6). In E. xix. we find that the giving of ·the law was in the third month after the departure from Egypt. The Israelites took their departure from Sinai in the second month of the second year (N. x. 11), and this was the time referred to in D. i. when these judges were appointed (v. 6, 9).

9. In D. x. 1–5, mention is made of the ark being prepared as a receptacle of the table of the laws before Moses goes up into the mount. The older narrative says nothing about an ark being prepared beforehand for the tables (E. xxxiv. 29). It is only after coming down with the second set of tables that Moses summons the wise-hearted (E. xxxv. 10–12) to "come and make all that the Lord hath commanded, the tabernacle, his tent and his covering, etc., the ark," etc. The tabernacle is constantly mentioned in the three middle books of the Pentateuch, but is never once named in Deuteronomy until the announcement to Moses in xxxi. 14, 15, that he should die. And this passage is shown to be an interpolation, with several others at the close of the book.

10. In D. x. 8, we read, "At that time the Lord separated the tribe of Levi," i. e., after the death of Aaron (v. 6). In N. iii. 5, 6, 7, the separation is made to take place in Aaron's lifetime.

11. The Deuteronomist lays great stress on the duty of being charitable and hospitable to the Levite, placing him in the same category as the stranger, the fatherless, and the widow, and treating him as a sort of mendicant when sojourning within the gates, thus ignoring the fact that the children of Levi were entitled to one-tenth in Israel for an inheritance (N. xviii. 21). Not a word is said about the Levites having any divine right to *demand* or at least to *accept* the payment of tithes from the people, according to the provisions supposed to have been made by Jehovah himself in N. xviii. 21. The Deuteronomist makes Moses speak of the Levite as an object of charity only a few months after the promulgation of this law in Numbers about the Levites' inheritance.

Not a trace of poverty in regard to the Levites is found in the first four books. Under the later kings we have unmistakable indications of the poverty of the priests.

12. In D. xiv. 19, every creeping thing that flieth is declared unclean, and is forbidden to be eaten. In L. xi. 21–23, every creeping thing that flieth is allowed to be eaten, and four forms of locusts are mentioned.

13. Numerous expressions common throughout the first four books are never employed by the Deuteronomist, and *vice versa*. Bishop Colenso cites thirty-three expressions in Deuteronomy, each of which is found on an average eight times in that book, but not one of which is found even once in the other four books. In Deuteronomy the expression "the Lord thy God," or "the Lord our God," occurs with remarkable frequency; but it is very rarely found in the other books.

WHEN WAS DEUTERONOMY WRITTEN, AND BY WHOM?

1. The author of Deuteronomy must have lived after the other writers of the Pentateuch, since he refers throughout to passages in the story of the exodus recorded in the other books, and refers directly, in xxiv. 8, to the laws about leprosy given in Leviticus. If, therefore, the Elohistic and Jehovistic portions of the Pentateuch were written not earlier than the times of Samuel, David, and Solomon, it is plain that the Deuteronomist must have lived no earlier, but probably later than the time of Solomon.

2. The phrase "sons of Levi" and "Levites," always used by the Deuteronomist, is invariably used by Jeremiah and the other later prophets (Jer. xxxiii. 18, 21, 22; Ezek. xliii. 19, xliv. 15, xlviii. 13; Mal. iii. 3. Comp. Mal. ii, 4, 8). The Deuteronomist, like Jeremiah, uses the word "law" in the singular only in speaking of the whole law (Jer. ii. 8, vi. 19, viii. 8, ix. 13). The Deuteronomist confines all sacrifices to the place where "Jehovah would place his name;" so Jeremiah speaks repeatedly of Jerusalem or the temple as a place called by Jehovah's name (vii. 10, 11, 14, 30, xxv. 29). Numerous other expressions are used by the Deuteronomist in common with the later Biblical writers only. Out of thirty-three expressions, each of which occurs on an average eight times in Deuteronomy, but not one of which is found in the other books of the Pentateuch, seventeen are found repeated with more or less frequency in Jeremiah, and many of the others

or their representatives are partially repeated in his prophecies, Expressions do occasionally occur in the other books of the Pentateuch which are peculiar to Deuteronomy ; but it is possible, if not probably, that the writer of the latter book may have interpolated those few passages.

3. The Deuteronomist, in xvii. 2–7, expresses strong abhorrence of all manner of idolatry, and especially of the worship of the " sun or moon, or any of the host of heaven," the first intimation of which worship is found in the reign of Josiah's father, Manasseh (2 K. xxi. 3, 5).

4. That the book of Deuteronomy was written after the time of Samuel is shown by the fact that the laws referring to the *kingdom* seem not to have been known to Samuel (1 S. viii. 6–18), nor to the later writer of Samuel's doings. In S. xii. 17–19, he charges it upon the people as a great sin that they had desired a king.

5. The mention of the kingdom in D. xvii. 14–18, with the distinct reference to the dangers likely to arise to the State from the king multiplying to himself " wives," " silver," " gold," and " horses," implies that the book was written after the age of Solomon ; and this is confirmed by the frequent reference to the place which Jehovah would choose, *i. e.*, Jerusalem and the temple.

6. The tabernacle, so frequently spoken of in the three middle books of the Pentateuch, but never once named by the Deuteronomist till near the close of the book, in an interpolated passage, had long since passed away in Jeremiah's time.

7. That the book was written after the captivity of the ten tribes, in the sixth year of Hezekiah's reign, is evident from the fact that the sorrows of that event are referred to as matters well known and things of the past (D. iv. 25–28).

8. In 2 K. xxii. and xxiii. we find an account of the discovery of the " book of the law in the house of the Lord," in the eighteenth year of King Josiah, which caused a great sensation. Where could this book have been hidden for eight centuries ? Could it have escaped the notice of David, Solomon, and others ? Can we resist the suspicion that the writing of the book and the placing of it where it was found were pretty nearly contemporaneous ? Shaphan, the scribe, read the book before the king, and appears to have read all the words of it. Again the

next day the king himself read in the ears of the people "all the words of the book of the covenant which was found in the house of the Lord." The name "book of the covenant" cannot well apply to all the Pentateuch, though it may apply to the book of Deuteronomy, or to the chief portion of it, since we find it written in D. xxix. 1, "These are the words of the covenant."

9. The whole description of the nature and effect of the words contained in the book shows that it must have been the book of Deuteronomy. A reform took place in regard to idolatrous practices immediately after the discovery of this book. Never before was such a passover held as in that same year; but we have no sign whatever of another such passover being held, even by Josiah. Perhaps after a time the young king also became aware of the real facts of the case, and his zeal may have been dampened by the discovery.

10. In that age and time of Jewish debasement, when the law book as it then existed was not well suited to the present necessities of the people, Jeremiah or any other seer may have considered himself justified in summoning up the spirit of the older law in a powerful address adapted to the pressing circumstances of the times, putting words into the mouth of the departed lawgiver, Moses, to reinforce the laws by solemn prophetical utterances. The intention may have been to put down by force the gross idolatries which abounded in the kingdom, through the influence of a disguised prophecy upon the mind of a well-meaning king.

11. The book of Deuteronomy must have been written after the great spread among the tribes of Canaan of the worship of the sun and moon and host of heaven (D. iv. 19). It seems to have been first generally practised in Judah in the reign of Manasseh, the father of Josiah (2 K. xxi. 3, 5; 2 Chr. xxxiii. 3). Manasseh's grandfather Ahaz may have introduced it, as appears from a comparison of 2 K. xxiii. 12; but it probably was not much practised, and it certainly was not adopted by his son Hezekiah. In Manasseh's reign, however, it seems to have flourished.

12. It must have been written before the time of Josiah's reformation, since the words ascribed to Huldah the prophetess, in D. xxii. 15–20, refer to it; for she says, "All the words of this book wherein the king hath read shall be fulfilled." She was probably in the secret, and shared the hope of a great reforma-

tion, and there is little doubt that the " book of the law " was the direct cause of that reformation. The whole theocratic state was in imminent danger from the idolatrous practices that were prevailing. So the Deuteronomist laid down a new set of laws in the name of Moses, and gave a new and firmer foundation to the theocratic state. The attempted reformation was not, however, successful, except to secure temple service at Jerusalem. That introduced dead formalism, which existed until the Israelitish nation became extinct.

13. It can scarcely be doubted, therefore, that it was written either in the latter part of Manasseh's reign or the early part of Josiah's. If it was written in the latter part of Manasseh's reign, the author must have lived, and probably have died, without seeing the result of his labor—without betraying his secret ; or, if he lived until the disclosure of it, it is difficult to account for his long silence with respect to its existence, which was maintained during seventeen years of Josiah's reign, when the king's docile piety and youth would have encouraged the production of such a book if it really existed, and there was such imperative necessity for that reformation to be begun as soon as possible, with a view to which the book was written. Thus it seems most reasonable to suppose that the book was in process of composition during the first seventeen years of Josiah's reign, when the youth of the prince and his willingness to follow the teachings of the prophets around him gave every encouragement for such an attempt being made to bring about the great change that was needed.

14. Jeremiah lived in that very age, and began to prophesy in the thirteenth year of Josiah, four or five years before this book was found.

IMMORAL COMMANDS OF DEUTERONOMY.

Bishop Colenso is glad to know that such commands as these, taken from this book, are at variance with God's law :

1. Excluding from the congregation of the Lord persons mutilated in helpless infancy, while those by whose agency the act in question was encouraged or perhaps performed are allowed free access to the sanctuary.

2. Excluding in like manner the innocent base-born child, but taking no account of the vicious parent.

3. Commanding the stubborn, rebellious son to be stoned to

death, when oftentimes the father and mother, who by their bad example had corrupted, or by their faulty training had ruined their child, deserved rather to suffer punishment.

4. Ordering that any city of any distant people with whom Israel might be at war should first be summoned to surrender, and if it should refuse to make peace on condition of all its inhabitants becoming tributary and doing service to Israel, it should then be besieged and every male thereof should be put to the sword ; while of the cities which Israel was to inherit they were to save nothing that breathed, lest they should become corrupted by their idolatries and abominations.

VOL. IV.

THE MOSAIC COSMOGONY.

In vol. IV., after a long preface devoted to answers to objections made to positions taken and supported in the previous volumes, Bishop Colenso proceeds to make a critical comparison of the Elohistic and Jehovistic passages in the first eleven chapters of Genesis, to show that they were composed by two distinct writers. The author then attacks the scientific and historical truthfulness of the Scripture cosmogony, making the following points:

THE SIX DAYS OF CREATION.

Despite all the criticisms of the word "create," the plain meaning of the first verse in Genesis is, that in the beginning of the six days, as the first act of that continuous six days' work about six thousand years ago, according to the Biblical chronology, God created the heaven and the earth. But geology teaches that the earth had existed millions of years before, and was brought into its present form by continual changes through a long succession of ages, during which enormous periods innumerable varieties of animal and vegetable life abounded, from a time beyond all power of calculation. So, also, God is represented as completing the work of creation in six literal days, and resting upon and sanctifying the seventh. In E. xx. 11, it is expressly said that " in six days God made the heaven and the earth, and all that in them is."

That they were not indefinite periods of time is further shown by the setting of two great lights in the firmament on the fourth day, to rule over the day and over the night, and to divide the light from the darkness. If the first three days were indefinite days, why is the same word in the Hebrew used for that portion of the twenty-four hours which the sun rules over? Is the sense of the word day, from the fourth day onward, to be considered different from that of the same word as used prior thereto?

THE ORDER OF CREATION.

The order of creation in Genesis is, first plants, then fish, then fowls, then cattle and reptiles, and lastly man. Geology shows that in the different ages plants and animals of all kinds appeared together at the same time on the earth; so that they were not successively created, as the Bible says, first *all the plants*, and then *all the fish*, etc.

CHAOS.

Genesis represents the earth as " without form and void," in a state of utter chaos and confusion, and wrapped in darkness, immediately before the races of plants and animals now existing on its face were created. Geology proves that the earth had existed generally just as now, with the same kind of animal and vegetable life as now, long before the six thousand years implied in the Bible story, and that no sudden convulsion took place at that time by which they might have been destroyed, so as to give occasion for a new creation.

THE SUN AND MOON CREATED ON THE FOURTH DAY.

It is a mere evasion of the plain meaning of words to say that God meant the sun and moon to *appear* first only on the fourth day, although they had been long before created—*appear*, that is, to the earth, when, however, according to the story, there was as yet no living creature on its face to see them! The writer uses the same Hebrew word "made" as he had used before when he says God *made* the firmament, and which he afterwards uses when he says God *made* the animals.

THE FIRMAMENT OF WATERS.

The dividing of the waters below the firmament from the

waters above it was founded upon the idea that the sky was an expanse, a spread-out surface, and that the upper waters dropped rain.

WHAT DID BEASTS OF PREY EAT?

To every animal God gave every green herb for meat. The question arises, how were the beasts of prey to be supported, since their teeth, stomachs, and bodily form were not adapted for eating herbs? But in fact geology teaches that ravenous creatures preyed on their fellow creatures, and lived on flesh, in all ages of the world's past history, just exactly as they do now. Besides, almost all fishes are carnivorous.

THE ZENDAVESTA STORY OF CREATION.

The account of the creation in Genesis corresponds with that of the Zendavesta, which was composed near the same locality. According to the latter, the universe was created in six periods of time by Ormuzd, in the following order: 1. The heaven and the terrestrial light between heaven and earth; 2. The water; 3. The earth; 4. The trees and plants; 5. Animals; 6. Man; whereupon the Creator rested and connected the Divine origin of the festivals with these periods of creation. The Persian tradition is substantially the same, showing that the story of Genesis had the same origin. It is an ancient myth.

ADAM FORMED OF DUST.

"And the Lord God formed man (Adam) of the dust of the ground" (Adamha). A play upon words.

THE RIVERS EUPHRATES, TIGRIS, NILE, AND INDUS UNITED.

The four rivers of Eden are made to unite in one. One of these rivers is the Euphrates, and there is but little doubt that the Hiddekel and the Gihon, as Josephus says, are the Tigris and Nile respectively, and Pison probably the Indus.

DEATH THREATENED FOR DISOBEDIENCE.

"In the day that thou eatest thereof thou shalt surely die." How could the first man understand what death was? He had not seen it.

NAMING OF THE ANIMALS.

Man was created before the other animals (the fishes excepted) according to the second chapter, and they were brought to Adam to be named. How could the white bear of the frozen zone and the humming bird of the tropics have met in one spot to be named, and then dispersed again ?

WAS EDEN THE CENTRE OF CREATION ?

Was there only one centre of creation ? Were all reptiles, fishes, and insects, as well as all plants, created in Eden only, and thence scattered to the ends of the earth ?—the Indian corn, for instance, which was not known in the eastern hemisphere until after the discovery of America ?

ORIGIN OF THE DIFFERENT HUMAN RACES.

It is even now an open scientific question whether the Australian savage, the African negro, the American Indian, and the Caucasian are all descendants of a first pair.

WOMAN MADE OUT OF A RIB.

The making of the woman out of the man's rib is thought by some to convey an idea of the intimate relationship, sacredness, and indissolubility of the conjugal state. The Greenlanders believe that the first woman was fashioned out of the man's thumb !

THE CUNNING SERPENT.

"Now the serpent was more subtle than any beast of the field." It is the Jehovistic interpolater who writes this passage. Here is the origin of evil, in a speaking serpent.

THE SERPENT CRAWLING AND EATING DUST.

"Upon thy belly shalt thou go, and dust shall thou eat." Here the serpent is represented as degraded and debased from what it was originally. But geology shows that it was the same kind of creature before man existed on the earth. As to the serpent's eating dust, it is a falsehood founded on the scantiness of its food. As to the enmity between the woman's seed and the serpent, it is not true. A snake is held in great respect among the Zulus. It was an emblem of healing wisdom among the Greeks, and a symbol of eternity to the Phœnicians.

PAIN IN CHILDBIRTH.

Pain to the woman in childbirth, and the subjection of woman to her husband, are fancies in the imagination of the Hebrew writer. The subjection of the female to the male is not peculiar to man amongst animals; and in tropical countries childbirth is attended with little more pain and disturbance than the birth of a beast.

CURSING THE GROUND.

"Cursed is the ground for thy sake." Geology shows no signs of any such curse. Thorns and briers were as plentiful in the primeval world as now ; and a life of toil and exertion is far more healthful and ennobling than one of indolence and inactivity.

RETURNING TO DUST.

"Till thou return unto the ground, for out of it thou wast taken." Geology shows that living creatures died long before. "For dust thou art, and unto dust shalt thou return." This would imply that Adam was not punished by death *for his sin*. Death of the body was regarded by the ancient writers as the end of all. No mention is made of the immortality of the soul.

PERSIAN STORY OF THE FIRST PAIR.

The Persian myth is similar to that of the Hebrews. The first couple, Meshia and Meshiana, lived originally in purity and innocence. Perpetual happiness was promised to them by the Creator. An evil demon (Dev) came to them in the form of a serpent, and gave them fruit of a wonderful tree, which imparted immortality. Consequently they fell and forfeited the eternal happiness for which they were destined. They killed beasts and clothed themselves; they built houses, but paid not their debt of gratitude to the Deity, and the evil demon obtained still more perfect power over their minds.

CHINESE STORY OF THE FALL.

The Chinese have their age of virtue, when Nature furnished abundant food, and man lived peacefully, surrounded by all the beasts, not knowing what it meant to do good or evil, and not subject to disease or death. But partly by an undue thirst for knowledge, and partly by increasing sensuality and the seduction of woman, he fell. Passion and lust ruled his mind, war with the animals began, and all Nature stood inimically arrayed against him.

PARADISE OF THE GREEKS.

The Greeks had their Paradise or Elysium—their garden of Hesperides, with its golden apples, in the islands of the blessed, guarded by ever-watchful serpents.

SACRED MOUNTAIN OF THE HINDOOS.

The Hindoos have their sacred mountain, Meru, in which no sinful man can exist. It is perpetually clothed in the golden rays of the sun, guarded by dreadful dragons, adorned by celestial plants, and watered by four rivers, which separate and flow in four directions.

WHO WAS TO KILL CAIN?

Cain is made to say, "Every one that findeth me shall slay me." The only man on the face of the earth was Adam; Seth was not yet born.

CAIN'S DESCENDANTS FAVORED.

The introduction of cattle-keeping, music, and smithery is ascribed to the descendants of Cain, on whom the curse had been pronounced!

LONGEVITY IN PREHISTORIC TIMES.

The great longevity of ancient times is common to the traditions of all nations. As soon as we come down to historical times we see no more of these great ages.

SONS OF GOD AND DAUGHTERS OF MEN.

"The sons of God saw the daughters of men." This is borrowed from foreign or heathen sources. See Book of Enoch—an acknowledged forgery.

ANCIENT GIANTS.

"There were giants in the earth in those days." The belief in races of giants was universal among the ancients, but that the stature of the human race was really the same generally in those days as now, is shown by the remains discovered in ancient tombs and pyramids.

STORY OF THE DELUGE.

In the story of the deluge the ark is made to rest on the highest summit of Ararat, and remain there seventy-three, or seventy-four days after the waters had retired from the earth. At this elevation of 17,000 feet—1,000 feet higher than Mont Blanc, and 3,000 feet above the region of perpetual snow—all the inhabitants of the ark must have frozen to death. Many other difficulties are presented and discussed, and in conclusion Colenso says that geology absolutely disproves the story.

WAS IT A PARTIAL DELUGE?

1. The difficulty of worms and snails crawling into the ark from some large terrestrial basin in western Asia, is just as great as from distant parts of the earth. One small brook would have been a barrier to further progress. Nor could Noah have provided for the wild carnivorous animals—the lion, leopard, eagle, vulture, etc. And what need to crowd the ark with birds which could easily have escaped beyond the boundaries of the inundation?

2. The language of the Bible is too sweeping. God says, "Every living substance that I have made will I destroy from off the face of the earth." (G. vii. 4.)

3. One volcanic region, forty miles by twenty, in the provinces of Auvergne and Languedoc, in France, contains deposits of scoria and lava extending over many miles, and in some places from fifty to one hundred feet deep, which must have taken many thousands of years to accumulate, and which have certainly not been submerged during at least eighteen thousand years past.

4. In all the diluvian deposits no trace of human remains has ever been found.

CHALDEAN STORY OF THE DELUGE.

Many heathen nations have traditions concerning a universal deluge. There is a Chaldean story of Xisthurus building an immense ship, 3,000 by 1,200 feet, loading it with provisions, entering it with his family and all species of quadrupeds, birds, and reptiles, and sailing toward Armenia. When the rain ceased he sent out birds to ascertain the condition of the earth. Twice they returned—the second time with mud on their feet. The third time they returned no more. By this time the ship had grounded on the side of an Armenian mountain, whereupon Xisthurus and his family left it, erected an altar, and offered sacrifices to the gods. Pieces of bitumen and timber, ostensibly taken from the ship, were in later times chiefly used as amulets.

GENERATIONS OF NOAH.

In G. **x.** the generations of Noah are enumerated. The nations of Eastern Asia are not enumerated at all, though the writer seems to have had some vague notion of the existence of distant families (*v.* 30).

IDENTITY OF LANGUAGE OF THE HEBREWS AND CANAANITES.

The fact that the patriarchs and Hebrews could converse with the surrounding nations shows that their language was common, and the indications are that the vernacular language of the Canaanites was substantially the same as that of the Hebrews. The language was radically the same from the earliest times.

THE HEBREW LANGUAGE, WHENCE DERIVED.

Whence was the Hebrew language derived? The fact that the Pentateuch was written in pure Hebrew appears to be strong if not positive proof of its having been written at a much later period of their national history than the exodus, or at a time when the language of Canaan had become, after several generations, the common tongue of the invading Hebrews, as well as of the heathen tribes which they drove out, and which they were unwilling to acknowledge as brethren. We never read of any interpreter between the Hebrews and the Philistines.

THE DISPERSION OF TONGUES.

The story of the dispersion of tongues is connected by the Jehovistic writer with the famous unfinished temple of Belus, of which probably some wonderful reports had reached him, in whatever age he may have lived. The derivation of the name Babel from the Hebrew word meaning *confound*, which seems to be the connecting point between the story and the tower of Babel, is altogether incorrect, the literal meaning of the word being *house*, or *court*, or *gate of Bel*.

REMARKABLE INCREASE IN FOUR HUNDRED YEARS.

In Abraham's time, not four hundred years after the deluge, the descendants of Noah's three sons, none of whom had a child before the deluge, had so multiplied that four kingdoms are mentioned as engaging in war against five other kingdoms (G. xv. 1, 2). Besides these there are a multitude of other nations named in the same chapter, some of which had attained a high state of civilization.

COMPLETE CHANGE OF PHYSICAL CHARACTER.

Moreover, in this short interval we find the most marked differences of physiognomy stamped on the different races, as shown on the ancient monuments of Egypt. There was a complete change of form, color, and general physical character, which seem not to have been modified during the four thousand years since.

NOAH'S UNDUTIFUL PROGENY.

Noah, and all the rest of Abraham's ancestors after Noah, were still living, as appears from the following record:

Noah			died 350	years after the flood.
Shem			" 502	" "
Arphaxad, born	2	years after, died 404	"	"..
Salah, ' "	37	"	" 470	"
Eber, "	67	"	" 351	"
Peleg, "	101	"	" 340	"
Reu, "	131	"	" 370	"
Serug, "	163	"	" 393	"
Nahor, "	193	"	" 341	" "
Terah, "	222	"	" 427	"
Abraham, "	292	"	" 467	" ..
Isaac, "	392	"	" 572	" "
Jacob, "	452	"	" 599	" "

And yet we do not find the slightest intimation that Abraham, Isaac, or Jacob paid any kind of reverence or attention to their illustrious ancestors.

ABRAHAM'S INCREDULITY ABOUT HAVING A SON.

Abraham laughed when told that a son should be born to him that was a hundred years old; and yet there were actually living those ancestors of his from one hundred and seventy to five hundred and eighty years old at the time. Shem was one hundred years old two years after the deluge, when he begat Arphaxad, and he lived thereafter five hundred years, and begat sons and daughters.

SILENCE OF THE REST OF THE OLD TESTAMENT ABOUT EDEN, THE FALL, AND THE DELUGE.

The fact that nowhere in the other books of the Old Testament is found any reference to the story in Genesis of the creation, or the fall of man, or the deluge, except in Isaiah liv. 9 (where the waters of Noah are mentioned), and Ezek. xiv. 14-20 (where the name of Noah is mentioned), is easy of explanation if the writer of these stories lived in the latter part of David's reign.

THE BOOK OF ENOCH.

In an appendix to vol. IV. the book of Enoch is examined. The Bishop says there is no doubt that the book is a fiction. According to Archbishop Laurence, it was composed within about fifty years immediately preceding the birth of Christ. From it most of the language of the New Testament, in which the judgment of the last day is described, appears to have been directly derived. It is full of such expressions and sentences as these : " Day of judgment." "Judgment which shall last forever." "Lowest depths of fire in torment." "Ancient of Days upon the throne of his glory." " The book of the living was opened in his presence " " Valley burning with fire." "Fetters of iron without weight." "Furnace of burning fire." "The word of his wrath shall destroy all the sinners and all the ungodly, who shall perish at his presence." "Trouble shall seize upon them when they shall behold this son of woman sitting upon the throne of his glory." " They shall fix their hopes on this son of man, shall pray to him and petition for mercy. Then shall the Lord of spirits hasten to expel them from his presence. Their faces shall be full of confusion, and their faces shall darkness cover. The angels shall take them to punishment that vengeance may be inflicted on those who have opposed his children and his elect. . . . But the saints and the elect shall be safe in that day. . . . The Lord of spirits shall remain over them, and with his son of man shall they dwell, eat, lie down, and rise up forever and ever."

VOL. V.

BOOK OF JOSHUA.

VOL. V. opens with an examination of the book of Joshua

after which the Bishop endeavors to separate the different por_ tions of the different writers of the Pentateuch and the book of Joshua, and to fix their exact age. The larger portion of the book of Joshua, he believes, is due to the Deuteronomist, who must consequently have lived at all events after the days of Moses, since the death and burial of Moses are recorded in D. xxxiv. The argument proceeds as follows:

THE DEUTERONOMIST.

Numerous expressions common to Deuteronomy and Joshua occur nowhere else in the Pentateuch. These Deuteronomistic formulas do not occur throughout the whole of the book of Joshua, but only in certain portions of it; in the remaining parts of the book, in which we find none of these formulas, we meet again with the peculiar phrases of the old writers of the Pentateuch which are never used by the Deuteronomist. The original lan_ guage has been retouched and blended with that of the Deuter- onomist. The same also is true of the other four books; there is plain evidence that the Deuteronomist has revised and retouched the manuscript before he added to it the sum and substance of the law of the book of Deuteronomy. More than half of the book of Joshua, especially of the historical and hortatory matter, consists of interpolations by the Deuteronomist.

RESEARCHES OF HUPFIELD AND BOEHMER.

The author gives a summary of the researches of Hupfield and Boehmer, exhibiting the Elohistic passages in Genesis, and showing great unanimity as the result of three independent re- searches. They all agree substantially, except in regard to four genealogical sections.

ELOHISTIC AND JEHOVISTIC PECULIARITIES.

There are more than one hundred different formulas or expres- sions, each of which occurs on an average more than ten times in Genesis, but only in those portions of it which remain when the Elohistic parts are removed. Some of them occur three times in one verse. On the other hand, the Elohistic portions in their turn exhibit their own phraseology, which is never repeated in the Jehovistic parts. Thus, only the Jehovistic portions contain such expressions as "lift up the eyes and see;" "lift up the voice and weep·" "fall on the neck and weep;" "find favor in the eyes of;" "see the face of;" "run to meet," etc.; and such words as "sin," "swear," "steal," "smite," "slay," "fear," "hate," "comfort," "embrace," "kiss," and even "love."

SIMPLICITY OF THE ELOHIST.

The Elohist appears to have had more correct views of the nature of the Divine Being and of his paternal relations to mankind, and less gloomy views of man's nature and the prospects of the human race. According to him, "God saw everything that he had made, and behold it was very good." But the Jehovist speaks of the earth as corrupt and filled with violence. The latter has a deep sense of sin and its consequences. The former knows nothing about the Garden of Eden, the forbidden fruit, the wily serpent, or the fall of man; it is only the Jehovist who multiplies curses upon the earth and pains of child-birth as the bitter consequences of our first parents' sin. The Jehovist gives all the darkest parts of the histories of indvidual life, such as the drunkenness of Noah, the presumption of the Babel builders, the great selfishness of Lot, the uncleanness of Sodom, the wickedness of Onan, etc. All those stories of impurity which make so many of the passages of Genesis totally unfit to be read in public or in the family are due to the Jehovist. The original Elohistic writer presents the character of the three patriarchs substantially without a flaw. It is the Jehovist who lowers them.

INTERPOLATIONS IN THE JEHOVISTIC NARRATIVE.

We have seen that there are interpolations in the original Elohistic narrative. We also find similar interpolations in different portions of the non-Elohistic matter itself. The non-Elohistic matter consists of the contributions of three or four different writers. For instance, chapter xiv. has no relation with any other part of Genesis. It brings Abraham before us in the character of a warlike Sheik, with 318 trained servants. But in the subsequent account of his going to Gerar (chap. xx.), where Abimelech takes his wife from him, Abraham is afraid of his life, and practises deceit, showing plainly that he could have had no such immense band of trained servants with him. He had routed the combined forces of Eastern kings, and needed not therefore, to have feared the power of the petty Prince of Gerar. This chapter contains four times the expression, "God most high," which occurs nowhere else in the Pentateuch, and only three times besides in the Bible—namely, in the Psalms.

THE DEUTERONOMIST AN EDITOR.

The later writer or Deuteronomist was not the compiler, but the editor of the Pentateuch and book of Joshua, which he interpolated throughout and enlarged, especially by the addition of the book of Deuteronomy. The interpolated passages for the most part seem to have been inserted for the purpose of quickening the history with a deeper spiritual meaning and stirring more effectually the reader's heart with words of religious life and earnestness. To this editor Colenso ascribes sixty-three verses entire of Genesis, and many more fragmentary notes.

FIRST AND SECOND ELOHIST.

About three-fourths of Genesis remain after removing the parts due to the second Jehovist and Deuteronomist. This three-fourths is so homogeneous in style that it is almost impossible to distingush the difference in style between the different sections of it except in one respect. There is a second Elohistic writer who uses decidedly Jehovistic formulas, though he has abstained from the use of the name Jehovah (Lord). But though it is difficult to separate the parts due to these two writers, Colenso has endeavored to do it. According to the critics there are five writers of the Pentateuch—namely, the Elohist, the Elohist number two, the Jehovist, the Jehovist number two, and the Deuteronomist. But Colenso thinks Elohist number two is the same as the Jehovist, only at an earlier period of his life. In his earliest attempts at interpolation he was perhaps somewhat stiff in style, which stiffness he overcame in his later years. Therefore the two may be identical.

HOW THE JEHOVIST REGARDED THE ELOHISTIC NARRATIVE.

It has been already shown in vol. II. that the first chapter of Genesis was written by the same hand which wrote Exodus v. 2-7, revealing the name of Jehovah to Moses. The Elohistic writer not having used that name until he used it in the above passage, intended to be understood that the name was unknown among men till then. Now if Moses himself really recorded that fact is it possible that other writers of his time would have dared to contradict it by interpolations? It is incredible. The interpolations must have been made at a later age by a writer who knew that the original record was not historically true, and therefore ventured to interpolate the name Jehovah. He must have known that the original narrative was a work of the imagination, and therefore that it was not necessary to adhere to the older statement.

AGE OF THE ELOHIST.

1. There is an air of primitive simplicity pervading the whole Elohistic story. The style is grave, prosaic, and unadorned. There is no instance of a story of indecency; crimes of violence are mentioned, but none of an indecent character.

2. According to the Elohist mankind first lived on vegetable food, and were not allowed to eat animals until after the flood.

3. In the Elohistic narrative there is no mention made of houses. The ark is the only exception, but the details of it—the dimensions, the door, the window, the roof, the stories—are given by the Jehovistic writer.

4. The Elohist makes no mention of sacrifices, priests, or tithes.

5. In G. xlviii. 5, 13, 14, Ephraim is set before Manasseh, though the latter was the first born, and both are reckoned as tribes of Israel. "As Reuben and Simeon they shall be mine." Now Manasseh was the most prominent among the Northern tribes until shortly before the time of Samuel, through its hero, Gideon (Jud. vi. 15). Hence the composition of Genesis cannot be assigned at an earlier period than about fifty years before Samuel, the time of Jephthah, nor later than the time of David, shortly after Samuel.

6. In S. xxxv. 11, God promises Jacob that "a nation and a company of nations shall be of thee, and kings shall come out of thy loins," No reference is made to his desccendants forming, as they did, two nations, Judah and Israel; but a nation is spoken of There is no enmity whatever implied in the Elohistic narrative between Joseph and his brethren. The children of Israel are plainly united in one body.

7. There is no enmity existing between Esau and Jacob—i. e., Edom and Israel; so that the narrative must have been written before the feeling between them became bitter, as recorded in 2 S. viii. 14. This brings the date to a time not later than Samuel.

8. "These are the kings that reigned in the land of Edom before there reigned any king over the children of Israel" (G. xxxvi. 31)

—meaning of course, all Israel, which restricts the time to that of Saul, David, and Solomon, the first three kings. But as the signs of a more primitive civilization in the narrative forbid our assigning it to the age of Solomon, or even the latter part of David's reign, we must refer it to the early part or the time of Samuel, when "all the Israelites went down to the Philistines to sharpen every man his share, and his coulter, and his ax, and his mattock;" and when "in the day of battle there was neither sword nor spear found in the hand of any of the people that were with Saul and Jonathan" (1 S. xiii. 20, 23).

9. The Elohist lays great stress on Hebron, in the land of Canaan, where the field of Machpelah lay, as the resting place of the bones of the Patriarchs. David, by Divine command, was directed (2 S. ii. 1) to make Hebron the centre of his power or seat of Government. He reigned in Hebron over Judah seven and a half years, and then in Jerusalem thirty-three years over Israel and Judah (2 S. v. 5). After this Hebron disappears from history altogether, except that Absalom begins his rebellion by asking leave to go and pay a vow unto the Lord in Hebron (2 S. xv. 7), and there sets up his kingdom (v. 10). It would seem highly improbable that all this importance should be ascribed to Hebron if the writer wrote after the first few years of David's reign, when he had captured the fortress of Zion and made Jerusalem his royal city (2 S. v. 6, 7).

10. Samuel lived three years after the anointment of David, and must have been aware of his valiant acts; and his hopes seem to have been centred in David after he had utterly despaired of Saul. He may have advised David to go to Hebron, and may have written the passages before us with a view to that event. Samuel, having most likely a band of young men under his training, had to provide instruction for them as a school of prophets. They had no Bible, no body of Divinity; and what is more likely than that he should have done his best to prepare such a narrative ?

AGE OF THE JEHOVIST.

1. The style of the Jehovist seems to be freer and easier than that of the second Elohist, thereby indicating a later authorship.

2. Extended geographical knowledge is exhibited, pointing to a later age than Samuel (G. ii. 11-14 and x.), when the people had

passed out of the mere agricultural condition in which they were living in the time of Samuel, and had begun to have freer inter-course with surrounding nations and more especially with the maritime people of Tyre and Sidon.

3. Indications of advanced civilization and even luxury are found in the Jehovistic portions (G. ii. 11, 12). Instruments of music and working in brass and iron are spoken of (iv. 21, 22), whereas in Saul's time " there was no smith found throughout all the land of Israel" (1 S. xiii. 19).

4. Considerable acquaintance with Egyptian affairs and customs is exhibited (xxxix. 20, xliii. 32, xlvi. 34, xlvii. 26, 1. 3).

5. Jacob is recorded as building himself a house (xxxiii. 17). The details of Noah's ark are similar to the directions for the tabernacle. There are indications of artistic skill of every kind which can scarcely have existed before the age of Solomon, and which in fact never was indigenous, but belonged to the Tyrian builders and other artisans engaged in the erection of the temple.

6. The hatred of Esau by Jacob is spoken of. In 2 K. viii. 20-22, we read of Edom revolting from under the hand of Judah. The prophecy in G. xxv. 23, that "the elder shall serve the younger," seems to have had its fulfilment in the latter part of David's reign, when Edom was crushed and did remain a servant to his younger brother Israel during the remainder of David's reign. But Edom recovered its independence at the beginning of Solomon's reign.

7. This would also explain another phenomenon in connection with this matter which we observe in the Jehovistic portion of Genesis—viz., the reconciliation of Esau and Jacob, and the generous conduct described in the narrative of chapter xxxviii.

8. The result remains that the Jehovistic sections of G. xxvii. 40, etc. referring to Esau, cannot have been written till after David's death, but were probably composed at the very beginning of Solomon's reign, when Edom had long been serving his brother and had just thrown off the yoke.

9. The Jehovist lays almost as much stress on Beer-sheba as the Elohist does on Hebron. Both Abraham and Isaac dig a well at Beersheba and acquire the right of possession in connection with a solemn covenant made with the Philistine king; whereas, according to the Elohist, each of the three patriarchs

lived solely at Hebron—at least after Abraham's acquisition of property there. And the Jehovist also in various places takes account of their having lived there at some time in their lives.

10. In the days of David and Solomon the Israelitish territory extended from Dan to Beersheba. The great stress laid on Beersheba therefore seems to point to the time of David and Solomon. The phrase "from Dan even to Beersheba" is first used in Jud. xx. 1, and in 1 S. iii. 20, narratives written, no doubt, in this age. It is afterwards repeated.

AGES OF THE DIFFERENT WRITERS.

The result of Colenso's researches is to fix the ages of the different writers, with the names of distinguished cotemporary prophets, as follows:

Elohist, . .	1100—1030 B. C., cotemporary prophet, Samuel
2d Elohist, } Jehovist, }	1060—1010 " " " Nathan.
2d Jehovist,	1035 " " " Gad.
Deuteronomist,	641—624 " " " Jeremiah.

Samuel may have begun the Elohistic story, and left it unfinished in the hands of his disciples, Nathan and Gad, whom we may fairly suppose to have been thrown under his auspices.

PHŒNICIAN ORIGIN OF THE NAME JEHOVAH.

The name Jehovah the author traces to the Phœnicians. They no doubt practiced substantially the same religion and spoke the same language as the Israelites. Most decisive proof is given of this by the series of Phœnician inscriptions lately published by the authorities of the British Museum. The great Phœnician Deity was the Sun, the male principle, while the Moon was regarded as the symbol of the co-operating recipient powers of nature, the female principle. The Sun was worshipped under a variety of names, among others that of Baal (Lord) and Adonis (my Lord). But there was one name more august and mysterious, employed chiefly at the great feast of the harvest, and expressed both by Christian and heathen writers by the very same Greek letters, by which they express also the mysterious Hebrew name. Thus there must have been a very close resemblance between the two names, and accordingly we find Phœnician names compounded with Jah exactly as Hebrew. It is preposterous to suppose that the Phœnicians derived their names from the Hebrews.

It is not necessary to suppose that the Elohist invented the name of Jehovah for his people. Samuel probably finding the tribes, the northern especially, already in possession of the name, adopted it as the name of the God of Israel. Afterwards the Deuteronomist breathed new life into the dead letter of the law. Meanwhile the people generally practised idolatry, even in the reign of David and Solomon. Jehosophat, Asa, Ahaziah, and Amaziah worshipped Jehovah (JHVH) on the high places, who was the Baal of Israel. There is no censure of the kings for allowing this idolatry by the writer of the books of Samuel and Kings. Yet all this while the great prophets of Israel were striving with their stolid and perverse countrymen, to raise their minds to higher views of the Divine nature, and nobler conceptions of the meaning of that name they were daily profaning.

CORRUPT WORSHIP OF JEHOVAH.

The worship of Jehovah being introduced among the Hebrews was long continued among them, as regards the great mass of the people, in the same low form in which it existed among the Canaanite tribes, and was only gradually purified from its grosser pollutions by the long continued efforts of those great prophets whom God raised up for the purpose from time to time in different ages, aided no doubt in this work by the powerful national calamities which befell them, and probably also in some measure by their coming in contact during the time of their captivity with those divine truths which were taught in the Zroasterian religion. In fact, the state of Israel may be compared with that which, in the view of many ardent Protestants, exists even now in Catholic communities. The people in such cases worship the same God as the Protestants; they call themselves Christians, servants of the same Lord, yet there is much in their religion which Protestant travelers regard as profound idolatry, and denounce as gross abominations.

THE NATION AND COUNTRY OF THE JEWS.

By W. H. B.

Very erroneous ideas prevail in regard to the magnitude of the nation and country of the Jews, and their importance in history. Most maps of ancient Palestine assign far too much territory to that nation. They make the greatest length of the country from 160 to 175 miles, and its greatest breadth from 70 to 90, inclosing an area of from 10,000 to 12,000 square miles—a little larger than the State of Vermont. They not only include the entire Mediterranean coast for 160 miles, but a considerable mountain tract on the north, above Dan, and a portion of the desert on the south, below Beersheba, besides running the eastern boundary out too far. Moreover, they lengthen the distances in every direction. From Dan to Beersheba, the extreme northern and southern towns, the distance on Mitchell's map is 165 miles, and on Colton's, 150; but on a map accompanying "Biblical Researches in Palestine," by Edward Robinson, D. D., which is one of the most recent and elaborate, and will doubtless be accepted as the best authority, the distance is only 128 miles.

Now, the Israelites were never able to drive out the Canaanites from the choicest portion of the country—the Mediterranean coast—nor even from most parts of the interior. (Judges i. 16-31 ; 1 Kings ix. 20, 21.) The Phenicians, a powerful maritime people, occupied the northern portion of the coast, and the Philistines the southern ; between these the Jebusites, or some other people, held control, so that the Israelites were excluded from any part of the Mediterranean shore. The map of their country must therefore undergo a reduction of a strip on the west at least 10 miles wide by 160 long, or 1,600 square miles. A further reduction must be made of about 400 square miles for the Dead Sea and Lake of Tiberias. This leaves at most 9,000 square miles by Colton's map. But on this map the extreme length of the country is 175 miles ; which is 47 miles too great; for the whole dominion of the Jews extended only from Dan to Beersheba, which Dr. Robinson places only 128 miles apart. We must therefore make a further reduction of an area about 47 by 60 miles, or 2,800 square miles. Then we must take off a slice on the east, at least 10 miles broad by 60 long, or 600 square miles. Thus we reduce the area of Colton's map, from 11,000 square miles, to 5,600—a little less than the State of Connecticut.

But now if we subtract from this what was wilderness and desert, and also what was at no time inhabited and controlled by the Israelites, we further reduce their habitable territory about one-half. The land of

Canaan being nearly all mountainous, and bounded on the south and east by a vast desert which encroached upon the borders of the country, a great part of it was barren wilderness. Nor did but one-fifth of the Is. raelites (two and a half tribes) occupy the country east of the Jordan which was almost equal in extent to that on the west, the proper land of promise. The eastern half, therefore, must have been but thinly popu. lated by the two and a half tribes, who were only able to maintain a precarious foothold against the bordering enemies. So then it is not probable that the Israelites actually inhabited and governed at any time, a territory of more than 3,000 square miles, or not much if any larger than the little State of Delaware. At all events, it can hardly be doubted that Delaware contains more good land than the whole country of the Jews ever did.

The promise to Abraham in Gen. xv. 18, is "from the river of Egypt to the river Euphrates." But the Jewish possessions never reached the Nile by 200 miles. In Ex. xxxiii. 31, the promise is renewed, but the river of Egypt is not named. The boundaries are "from the Red Sea to the Sea of the Philistines (the Mediterranean), and from the desert to the river." By "the river" was doubtless meant the Euphrates; and assuming that by "the desert" was meant the eastern boundary (though Canaan was bounded on the south also by the same great desert, which reached to the Red Sea), we have in this promise a territory 600 miles long by an average of about 180 broad, making an area of about 100,000 square miles, or ten times as much as the Jews ever could claim, and nearly one-half of it uninhabitable. So then the promise was never ful- filled, for the Israelites were confined to a very small central portion of their land of promise, and whether they occupied 3,000 or 12,000 square miles in the period of their greatest power, tho fact is not to be disputed that their country was a very small one.

What was the physical character of the land of Canaan? It is de- scribed in the Pentateuch as a "land flowing with milk and honey." Such it may have seemed to the Israelites after wandering forty years through the frightful desert of Sinai and Edom, where but for tho miraculous supply of food and water, every soul of them would have per- ished. But what was there in Canaan to warrant so extravagant an enco- mium? Surely there are no signs there now of its ever having been even a fertile country. Modern travelers all agree that it is very barren and desolate. How could it bo otherwise? It is a country of rocks and mountains, and is bounded on two sides by a vast desert.

Lamartine describes the journey from Bethany to Jericho as singularly toilsome and melancholy—neither houses nor cultivation, mountains without a shrub, immense rocks split by time, pinnacles tinged with colors like those of an extinct volcano. "From the summit of these hills, as far as the eye can reach, we see only black chains, conical or broken peaks, a boundless labyrinth of passes rent through the mountains, and those ravines lying in perfect and perpetual stillness, without a stream, without a wild animal, without even a flower, the relics of a convulsed land, with waves of stone." (Vol. II., p. 146.)

But lest it may be thought that these dismal features are due to modern degeneracy, let us take the testimony of an early Christian father, St. Jerome, who lived a long time in Bethlehem, four miles south of Jerusalem. In the year 414 he wrote to Dardanus thus:—

" I beg of those who assert that the Jewish people after coming out of Egypt took possession of this country (which to us, by the passion and resurrection of our Saviour has become truly the land of promise), to show us what this people possessed. Their whole dominions extended only from Dan to Beersheba, hardly 160 Roman miles in length (147 geographical miles). The Scriptures give no more to David and Solomon, except what they acquired by alliance, after conquest. . . . . I am ashamed to say what is the breadth of the land of promise, lest I should thereby give the pagans occasion to blaspheme. It is but 47 miles (42 geographical miles) from Joppa to our little town of Bethlehem, beyond which, all is a frightful desert." (Vol. II., p. 605.)

Elsewhere he describes the country as the refuse and rubbish of nature. He says that from Jerusalem to Bethlehem there is nothing but stones, and in the summer the inhabitants can scarcely get water to drink.

In the year 1847, Lieut. Lynch, of the U. S. Navy, was sent to explore the river Jordan and the Dead Sea. He and his party with great difficulty crossed the country from Acre to the lake of Tiberias, with trucks drawn by camels. The only roads from time immemorial were mule paths. Frequent detours had to be made, and they were compelled actually to make some portions of their road. Even then the last declivity could not be overcome, until all hands turned out and hauled the boats and baggage down the steep places; and many times it seemed as if, like the ancient herd of swine, they would all rush precipitately into the sea. Over three days were required to make the journey, which, in a straight line would be only 27 miles. For the first few miles they passed over a pretty fertile plain, but this was the ancient Phenician country, which the Jews never conquered. The rest of the route was mountainous and rocky, with not a tree visible, nor a house outside the little walled villages. (pp. 135 to 152.)

Arriving at the ancient sea of Galilee, they purchased the only boat owned there (Letter to the Secretary of State). On this insignificant body of water, 12 miles long by 7 wide, all the commerce of the Jews was carried on, except in the reign of Solomon, when they had the use of a port on the Red Sea. From thence, the party proceeded down the Jordan; some in boats, the rest by land. They had to clear out old channels, make new ones, and sometimes, trusting in Providence, they plunged with headlong velocity down appalling descents. On the third morning the frame boat was smashed and abandoned. The metallic boats which they had provided for this perilous voyage were the only kind that would survive. They plunged down twenty-seven threatening rapids, besides many smaller ones in their passage from the lake to the Dead Sea, a distance of 200 miles by the crooked Jordan, but only 56 in a straight line. The fall in the whole distance is 634 feet. The width of the river, Lieut. Lynch says, was 75 feet; but as this was at the time of the flood, it must have been much less at low water. Other travelers say it is only 40 feet wide. Even as it was, their boat, drawing only eight inches of water, grounded in mid-channel, showing how very shallow the river must have been in summer. A bridge spanning the stream with a single pointed Saracenic arch is described by Lieut. Lynch, and a drawing of it is given by the Rev. Mr. Tristram in his "Land of Israel" (London, 1865) Through this single arch the waters have rushed for centuries, and still the bridge endures. Such is the famous Jordan—a narrow, shallow, crooked, impetuous mountain stream.

In a book entitled "The Holy Land, Syria," etc., by David Roberts, R. A. (London, 1855), the valley of the Jordan is thus described:—

"A large portion of the valley of the Jordan has been from the earliest time almost a desert But in the northern part, the great number of rivulets which descend from the mountains on both sides, produce in many places a luxuriant growth of wild herbage. So too in the southern part, where similar rivulets exist, as around Jericho, there is even an exuberant fertility; but those rivulets seldom reach the Jordan, and have no effect on the middle of the Ghor. The mountains on each side are rugged and desolate; the western cliffs overhanging the valley at an elevation of 1,000 or 1,200 feet, while the eastern mountains fall back in ranges of from 2,000 to 2,500 feet."

From the mouth of the Jordan to Jerusalem, the elevation is 3,927 feet. The distance in a straight line on Robinson's map is 16 miles. From the nearest point on the Dead Sea it is 12 1-2 miles. An air-line railroad, therefore, from the mouth of the river to Jerusalem would require an average grade of 245 feet to the mile; and from the nearest point on the Dead Sea, 314 feet to the mile. The length of the route would have to be more than doubled or trebled to make a railroad practicable. From Jerusalem to Yafa, the nearest practicable point on the Mediterranean, is 33 miles in a direct line. As Jerusalem is 2,610 feet higher than the sea level, the average grade of an air-line railroad between the two places would be about 80 feet per mile. Should the time ever come when a railroad would be required from the Mediterranean to the river Jordan, via Jerusalem, the question might arise, which would be the most practicable—the heavy grades required, or a tunnel from ten to twenty miles long, and from one to two thousand feet below the site of the holy city.

What was the size of ancient Jerusalem? We know pretty nearly what it is now, and how many inhabitants it contains. It is three-quarters of a mile long, by a half a mile wide, and its population is not more than 11,500 (*Biblical Researches*, Vol. I., p. 421), a large proportion of whom are drawn thither by the renowned sanctity of the place. Dr.

Robinson measured the wall of the city, and found it to be only 12,978 feet in circumference, or nearly two and a half miles. (Vol. I., p. 268.).

In a book entitled "An Essay on the Ancient Topography of Jerusalem," by James Fergusson (London, 1847), a diagram is given of the walls of ancient and modern Jerusalem, from which it appears that the greatest length of the city was at no time more than 6000 feet, or a little more than a mile, and its greatest width about three-quarters of a mile; while the real Jerusalem of old was but a little more than a quarter that size. The author gives the area of the different walled inclosures as follows (p. 52):—

Area of the old city, - - - - - - 513,000 yards.
That of the city of David, - - - - 243,000
                                                          ———————
Partial Total, - - - - - - 756,000
That inclosed by the wall of Agrippa, , - - 1,456,000
                                                          ———————
Grand total, - - - - - - 2,212,000

With these measurements Mr. Fergusson undertakes to estimate the probable population of the ancient city, as follows:—

"If we allow the inhabitants of the first named cities fifty yards to each individual, and that one-half of the new city was inhabited at the rate of one person to each one hundred yards, this will give a permanent population of 23,000 souls. If on the other hand we allow only thirty-three yards to each of the old cities, and admit that the whole of the new was as densely populated as London; or allowing one hundred yards to each inhabitant, we obtain 37,000 souls for the whole—which I do not think it at all probable that Jerusalem ever could have contained as a permanent population."

In another part of the book (p. 47) he says :—

"If we were to trust Josephus, he would have us believe that Jerusalem contained at one time, or could contain, two and a half or three millions of souls, and that at the siege of Titus, 1,100,000 perished by famine and the sword; 97,000 were taken captive, and 40,000 allowed by Titus to go free "

In order to show the gross exaggeration of these numbers, he cites the fact that the army of Titus did not exceed, altogether, 30,000, and that Josephus himself enumerates the fighting men of the city at 23,400, which would give a population something under 100,000. But even this he believes to be an exaggeration. For says he:—

"In all the sallies it cannot be discovered that at any time the Jews could bring into the field 10,000 men, if so many. . . . . Titus inclosed the city with a line four and one half miles in extent, which, with his small army, was so weak a disposition that a small body of the Jews could easily have broken through it; but they never seem to have had numbers sufficient to be able to attempt it."

The author guesses that the Jews might have mustered at the beginning of the siege about 10,000 men, and that the city might have contained altogether about 40,000 inhabitants, permanent and transient, in a space which in no other city in the world could accommodate 30,000 souls. But the wall of Agrippa was built, as this same author states, twelve or thirteen years after the crucifixion ; hence prior to that time the area of Jerusalem was only 756,000 yards, and it was capable of containing only 23,000 inhabitants at most, but probably never did contain more than 15,000.

Now Jerusalem was the chief city of the Jews, and the greatest extent of territory occupied by that nation does not now contain more than 200,000 inhabitants, if as many. Allowing to Jerusalem, in the period of the greatest prosperity of the Jews, a population of even 20,000, is it at all probable that the whole country could have contained anything like even the lowest estimate to be gathered from the Scripture record? In 1 Chr. xxi. 5, 6, we read that the number of " men that drew the sword " of Israel and Judah, amounted to 1,570,000, not counting the tribes of Levi and Benjamin. In 2 Samuel xxiv. 9, the number given at the same census is 1,300,000, and no omission is mentioned. Assuming the larger number to be correct, and adding only one-eighth for the two tribes of Levi and Benjamin, which may have been the smallest, we have 1,766,000 fighting men. This would give, at the rate of one fighting man to four inhabitants, a total population of over 7,000,000 souls. But if we adopt a more reasonable ratio, of one to six, we have a population of over 10,500,000 souls. And then we omit the aliens. These numbered 153,600 working men only two years later (2 Chr. ii. 17), and the total alien population, therefore, must have been about 500,000, which, added to the census, would make the total population from 7,500,000 to 11,000,000, or more. Can any intelligent man believe that a mountainous, barren country, no larger than Connecticut, without commerce, without manufactures, without the mechanical arts, without civilization, ever did, or could subsist even two millions of people ? Much less can it be believed that it subsisted " seven nations greater and mightier than the Israelitish nation itself" (Deut. vii. 1), i. e., not less than 14,000,000.

That the Jews were a very barbarous people is undeniable. Assuming as true, the account of their remarkable battle with the Midianites prior to their entrance into Canaan, the wholesale slaughter of men, women and children was an act peculiar only to a savage people. Who but a barbarian chief could have commanded the murder in cold blood by the returning victors, of all their captive women and children, save 32,000 virgins whom they were to keep alive for themselves!

Again, on taking the town of Jericho, they massacred all its inhabitants, saving only the harlot Rahab, who by falsehood and treachery had betrayed her own people.

Sometime afterwards a civil war broke out among the Israelites themselves, in which the tribe of Benjamin was almost exterminated, leaving only 600 males; whereupon the people, unwilling that one of their tribes should be annihilated, fell upon and sacked a whole city of another of their tribes, killing all its inhabitants except the virgins whom they gave for wives to the survivors of the tribe of Benjamin. The Benjamites lost in that battle 26,100 men, and their adversaries 40,030. (Judges xx. 15, 21, 25, 31.) The latter, however, not content with slaughtering all the Benjamites but 600, proceeded to their towns and slew every man, woman and child of the tribe. These must have numbered at least 80,000; so that the whole number killed in the three days of fratricidal warfare was not less than 146,000.

Slavery necessarily makes a people barbarous. Not only were the Israelites a nation of slaves, according to their own record, but after their entry into Canaan, they were six times reduced to bondage in their own land of promise. During a period of 281 years, they were in slavery 111 years, viz:—

Under the King of Mesopotamia, - 8 years. (Judges, iii. 8.)
Under the King of Moab, - - 18 " (" iii. 14.)
Under the King of Canaan, - - 20 " (" iv. 3.)
[Under the Midianites, - - - 7 " (" vi. 1.)]
In Gilead, - - - - - 18 " (" x. 8.)
Under the Philistines, - - - 40 " (" xiii. 1.)

That the Jews were far behind their surrounding neighbors in civilization is shown by the fact that in the first battle they fought under their first king, Saul, they had in the whole army "neither sword nor spear in the hand of any of the people," except Saul and Jonathan. (1 Samuel xiii. 22.) Nor was any "smith found throughout all the land of Israel" (.v 19), but "all the Israelites went down to the Philistines to sharpen every man his share, and his coulter, and his ax, and his mattock." (v. 20.) This was 404 years after the exodus, and only 75 years prior to the building of Solomon's temple. Their weapons of war were those of the rudest savage. David used a sling to kill Goliath, showing that he had not yet learned the use of more civilized weapons; not even the bow, which he afterwards caused to be taught to his people. (2 Samuel i. 18.)

As another evidence of the barbarism of the Jews, when David resolved to build a house for himself, he had no native artisans, but had to send to Hiram, King of Tyre, for masons and carpenters. (2 Samuel v. 11.) Even the wood itself had to be brought from Tyre. It would seem that even in those days, as now, the mountains of Canaan were destitute of trees—a sure sign of a sterile country. The wood of course had to be carried over land. Wheel-carriages were unknown to the Israelites, except in the form of chariots of iron used by their enemies, which prevented Judah, even with the help of the Lord, from driving out the inhabitants of the valleys. (Judges i. 19.) David captured 1,000 chariots in about the 16th year of his reign, of which he preserved only 100, disabling all the horses. (1 Chr. xviii. 3.) Prior to this event neither chariots nor horses had been used by the Israelites, nor was much use made of them by the subsequent kings. Oxen and asses were their beasts of burden; camels were rare even long after Solomon's reign. How then was the wood brought from Tyre over the mountains, unless it was carried on the backs of oxen or asses, or dragged along the ground?

The national wealth seems to have increased prodigiously in David's reign—chiefly from spoils—but the amount is manifestly greatly exaggerated. Among his spoils was the crown of the King of Rabbah, the weight of which was a talent of gold (2 Samuel xii. 30) ; *i. e.*, 93 3-4 pounds avoirdupois—a pretty heavy burden for a royal head. At the beginning of his reign, David had not even iron with which to forge weapons of war or implements of agriculture, and yet after forty years it is said that he left to his son Solomon, for the temple, 3,000 talents of gold and 7,000 of silver. (1 Chr. xxix. 4.) Now a talent of gold, according to the " table of weights and money " in the Bible, published by the American Bible Society, is equal to 5,464*l*. 5*s*. 8 1-2*d*., or $26,447 ; and a talent of silver is equal to 341*l*. 10*s*. 4 1-2*d*., or $1,653. The amount of gold and silver, therefore, which David contributed was equal to $90,912,000. But this is not all. The chiefs, princes, captains, and rulers over the King's work gave 5,000 talents, and 10,000 drachms of gold, and 10,000 talents of silver (*v.* 7),—equal to $153,845,000. So that the total sum of gold and silver contributed by David and his chiefs was $244,757,000, besides precious stones and an incredible quantity of brass and iron. Can it be believed that David and his men acquired such riches that they were able to make these enormous contributions?

In the reign of Solomon gold and silver continued to pour in so that he was able to buy a fleet of ships in the Red Sea, of Hiram, King of Tyre, and these ships brought him from Ophir 450 talents of gold, as we read in 2 Chr. viii. 18—equal to about $12,000,000—though in 1 Kings ix. 28, the amount given is 420 talents, or about $800,000 less. Again, we read in 1 Kings x. 14, that the weight of gold that came to him in one year was 666 talents—equal to about $18,000,000. And yet this same monarch, who " exceeded all the Kings of the earth for riches " (*v.* 23), had neither wood, nor skilled workmen to build his palace and temple, but bought the wood and hired the artisans of the King of Tyre. (2 Chr. ii. 3-10 ; 1 Kings v 6-12.) The laborers employed in the Temple were all the strangers in the land, numbering 153,000, of whom 3,600 were made overseers. (2 Chr. ii. 17, 18.) Over these were set 550 Jewish overseers according to 1 Kings ix. 33, or 250 according to 2 Chr. viii. 10. With this great number of workmen, Solomon was seven years in building this celebrated Temple, which was only 110 feet long, 36 wide, and 55 high. (1 Kings vi. 2.) How many a modern church edifice exceeds in size Solomon's great Temple ! But there were additions to the house. First, there was a porch at one end 36 feet by 18 (*v.* 3). This porch is said, in 2 Chr. iii. 4, to have been 220 feet high, or four times the height of the house! But as nothing is said about the hight of it in Kings, we may assume that the chronicler made a mistake in his figures in this case, as he has so frequently done in others. Then there were added to the walls of the house outside chambers, nine feet high, and from nine to thirteen feet broad, in three tiers, making a hight of 27 feet. But even with these additions, the temple was not remarkable for size, and the story that 150,000 laborers were employed seven years in its construction, is incredible.

So, too, as regards the amount of the precious metals said to have been used in the building of the Temple, it is fabulous. The quantity of gold alone which David and his chiefs are said to have given, would weigh 750,000 pounds avoirdupois, or 375 tons—enough of itself to cover the building outside and in, with a plate of gold weighing ten pounds to the square foot, and then leave over 100 tons for the inner and outer chambers, and all the paraphernalia—quite enough for the purpose, if economically used, without touching the 796 tons of silver.

On the death of Solomon a division took place among the tribes, the kingdom was torn asunder and divided into two small provinces, called Judah and Israel ; two and a half tribes composing the former, and nine and a half the latter. A religious war broke out between the two kingdoms, and while it was going on the kings of Assyria came down upon the nine and a half tribes and carried them away captive. The captives never returned, nor can any one to this day tell where they were dispersed. The small remnant of the Jews soon after became a prey to conquerors and were carried captive to Babylon. The captivity of the two and a half tribes took place 588 years B. C., and was practically an end of the Jewish nation. They were slaves in Babylon and its vicinity, till 536 years B. C. (Ezra i. 1–6), a period of 52 (not 70) years, when they were released by Cyrus and allowed to return to Judea. But it appears that less than 50,000 returned. (Ezra ii. 64, 65.) These, no doubt, were of the poorer class, the wealthier remaining in Babylon, and contributing alms for the rebuilding of the city of Jerusalem and the Temple. The amount contributed, according to Ezra ii. 68, 69, was 61,000 drachms of gold, and 5000 pounds of silver—equal in the aggregate to about $110,000 ; but according to Nehemiah vii. 70, 72, it was 41,000 drachms of gold and 4,200 pounds of silver—equal to about $290,000. Whichever was the correct amount, it was not a 600th part of what David and his men contributed for the first temple.*

About eighty years later, further contributions were made, amounting

---

* These two chapters, Ezra ii. and Nehemiah vii. are almost exactly alike, the whole of the former being repeated in the latter, with slight variations. Both give the names of the families that returned, and the number of each. They agree in making the whole number 42,360, besides 7,337 servants ; but on casting up the separate numbers, the whole sum in Ezra is 29,818 ; and in Nehemiah 31,089. Again, on comparing the two chapters verse by verse, we find twenty-seven discrepancies in figures, and thirty in names.

to nearly $4,000,000 (only a 60th part of what David and his men gave), and sent by Ezra with a guard of about 1,750 men from Babylon to Jeru_ salem. (Ezra viii.) But the effort to re-establish the Jewish nation proved futile. Though they were permitted in some degree to establish their superstitious religious rites in their former country, they were ever af_ terwards the subjects of other powers. until their final dispersion at the siege of Jerusalem, by Titus, A. D 70. For half a century after its destruction, says Dr. Robinson, there is no mention of Jerusalem in his_ tory; and even until the time of Constantine its history presents little more than a blank. (Vol. I., pp. 367, 371.)

Such was the insignificance of the Jews as a people, that the historical monuments preceding the time of Alexander the Great, who died 323 years B. C., make not the slightest mention of any Jewish transaction. The writings of Thales, Solon, Pythagoras, Democritus, Plato, Herodotus, and Xenophon, all of whom visited remote countries, contain no mention of the Jews whatever. Neither Homer, the cotemporary of Solomon, nor Aristotle, the correspondent of Alexander, makes any mention of them. The story of Josephus, that Alexander visited Jerusalem, has been proved to be a fabrication. Alexander's historians say nothing about it. He did pass through the coast of Palestine, and the only re_ sistance he encountered was at Gaza, which was garrisoned by Persians. (*Wyttenbach's Opuscula*, Vol. II., pp. 416, 421.)

Soon after the death of Alexander, the Jews first came into notice under Ptolemy I. of Egypt, and some of their books were collected at the new-built city of Alexandria. But they remained an obscure people, so much so that when Christ was crucified in the province of Judea under the Roman government, no record of the event seems to have been reg_ istered in the archives of that great empire; for if any had been, it would doubtless have heen preserved, at least for 300 years, and pro_ duced by the Emperor Constantine, the first royal pagan convert to Chris_ tianity, in his oration before the council of Nicæa, A. D. 326, on the evi_ dences of the Christian religion.

Persecution has probably made the Jews in modern times more numer_ ous than they ever were as an ancient nation. Little reliance can be placed upon their early history, which is entirely unsupported by cotem_ porary records. The story of their origin is doubtless fabulous. It is more probable that they were at first a wandering tribe of Bedouin Arabs who got possession of the sterile portion of Palestine, and held it until it was pretty thoroughly ruined. At all events it is clear that their im_ portance has been unduly magnified.

CPSIA information can be obtained
at www.ICGtesting.com
Printed in the USA
LVOW08s0339080517

533667LV00013B/148/P